Christian Bass

THIS IS ME, A MONKEY IN THE MUSIC

Is it possible that a photographer is hiding beyond a journalist? A writer beyond a photographer? And beyond a drop-out someone who's quite willing to have a career - but by his own rules and at his own time and place?

Can a man from Hamburg, Germany survive in Mauritius, Africa? And what's going on in such a man?

Many questions surround writer, photographer and journalist Christian Bass. In "This is me, a monkey in the music" he answers them all. He invites his readers to have a close look at his inner thoughts and fears. In his lyrics he talks about his ups and downs.

"This is me!" is a simple but self-confident statement of a man who has proven "If you really want something, there's always a way!"

PRELUDE

Lucky. There's no better word to describe how I feel about this collection. Lucky—and yeah, maybe a little proud—that you're here with me, and that I get to share the fourth edition of *This is me, a monkey in the music* with you.

What's changed? Honestly, not a lot. I've shuffled the lyrics around, thrown in some new poems, and totally revamped the layout. It's more like what I imagined when I first put this book together—a bit of a facelift to match the original vision.

I hope you enjoy this short trip through my past. We'll be making stops at a few key moments in my life—some fun, some not so much. But there's always a truth hidden in there. Just like the first time I shared *This Is Me*, it still feels a bit weird. You're about to get a much deeper look into who I am. You'll step into my past, into my safe space. And if I'm honest, that's not exactly something I'm comfortable with. But it's important. I know it is.

So, here's my invitation to you—come on in.

Welcome to my world!

WHO AM I?

Who am I and who could I be?
Questions with no meaning at all
The right answer depends on me
Who am I and who could I be?
Nobody unless I am free
Sometimes I stand, sometimes I fall
Who am I and who could I be?
Questions with no meaning at all!

STRUGGLING WITH LIFE

Back in time I see this boy struggling with his life
Filled with dreams and high hopes; he fights to stay alive
His demons, his secret, lost in his own conflict
Not a boy yet a man, feeling betrayed and tricked
While he spent his childhood on the Hollywood Drive
Just his dreams of the Broadway let this boy survive
Turned his blues into a rocking mid-summer-night jive
Gave him a reason and answered why he got picked
Struggling with his life
His parents already were looking for a wife
A good decent woman that makes his name survive
Between duty and his loving heart he felt kicked
Disgusted with which future his parents have picked
Out of options for truth would hit them like a knife
Back in time I see myself struggling with my life!

PART ONE

This is me, a monkey in the music

THE MONKEY IN THE MUSIC

One day I'll return to the place
where my heart feels at home,
Where I was young and innocent
and never spent a day alone.

Here I am! After six long years, the "monkey in the music" found its way home. Back in 2002/2003, when I wrote **Starting Something... Again**, I was sure it marked the beginning of a change—a shift from being a kid to finally growing up. I even felt it in my lyrics. The world seemed wide open, and I thought nothing could stand in my way. I had no idea I was about to tumble headfirst into a nightmare.

The ideas in my head, once crisp and clear, fell apart the moment I put pen to paper. It was like everything I tried to create turned to dust. The harder I pushed, the worse it got. My writing — my lifeline, my therapy — just disappeared. The words that once flowed like music were gone. And with them, my soul started to crack. Every time I thought I hit rock bottom, the floor just dropped out from under me again. I fought hard. Despair became my shadow. I did everything I could to break through that wall, until finally, I gave in. Defeated. It felt like fate had spoken.

But then, like flipping a switch, things changed. Maybe my batteries had recharged, or maybe I finally had something real to say. For a long time, I'd toyed with the idea of writing my biography. Something raw, something real, that let people in deeper than **Starting Something... Again** ever could.

I made a few false starts. None of them worked out, but I wasn't worried. I was in love, had a plan for the future, and felt a freedom I hadn't known before. I knew, in time, the right words would come. I gave up my apartment, dove into journalism, and spent my days wrapped up in bed with my boyfriend. Life was good.

Then 2009 hit. My boyfriend and I drifted apart, and someone new came into my life. For the first time, I was head-over-heels in love. We messaged non-stop, and soon we decided it was time to meet. I hadn't taken a vacation in over a decade, so I booked a trip to see him in Mauritius. Just before the flight, I wrote *Life's Too Short*, a kind of final farewell — just in case that plane decided to drop out of the sky.

Mauritius was paradise. After two perfect weeks, I returned to Germany for my sister's wedding—finally tying the knot with her childhood love. Not long after that, I was back on a plane to Mauritius for another month. That's when my boyfriend and I made the call: we were moving in together. My plan to move to Mauritius was set.

New Year's rolled around, and I was engaged, counting down my last two months in freezing Germany. The snow piled up, but inside, something had changed. I started writing again. The chorus and first verse of *This Is Me* spilled out. And since I was back in the flow, I made a little booklet for my family, showing off pictures of my new life in Mauritius. I wrote *Ocean Dream* for them. Suddenly, I couldn't stop writing. It took a while for me to realize it, but ***This is me, a monkey in the music*** was my comeback. Not some anthology of my wasted youth's lyrics, but the real deal.

So here we are, ready to peel back the mask, dig into the story of how I found my way to this ocean dream. The angel of the past? Gone. Won't ever come back. But I've learned over the years—nothing feels better than blood on blood.

There are still questions to answer, ones that'll help make sense of my life. Why did they do it? I don't have the answer yet, but I'm betting we'll find clues hidden between the lines.

And let's be real—would it be wrong to hope that creativity stays by my side? The kid who once hated being called a son of Hamburg is still here, even though it's true.

I've made my peace with the past. Life's too short, and now I know that for sure. So, I'm proud to say that we're back. Back to travel through my story, together. I hope you enjoy this journey as much as I do.

This is me and I am real!
This is me and I am me, finally!

(Pereybere, Mauritius, 2011)
Christian Bass

THIS IS ME

This is me, here I am, mighty glad that you came
With you on my side, life will never be the same
This is me; here I stand, simply the man I am
Back from hell and out on the road of life again
This is me, glad to say, finally on my way

The sun is burning on my skin, while the years are passing by
Once so close faces, drawn into the stream of tides
The first kiss and then the first love that made a happy boy cry
The moments of anger; the joy when I was right
Everything seemed to be like yesterday, then so far away
Still the kids we were, laughing and fighting nearly every day

This is me, here I am, mighty glad that you came
With you on my side, life will never be the same
This is me, here I stand, simply the man I am
Back from hell and out on the road of life again
This is me, glad to say, finally on my way

The waves are whispering near me, while my past is still alive
Once so big events, long forgotten by now
The first word and then the first rhyme
This helped a boy to survive
The feeling of success, the spotlight of the show
Everything seemed to be like yesterday, then so far away
Just a memory, fading out with every following day

This is me, here I am, mighty glad that you came
With you on my side, life will never be the same
This is me; here I stand, simply the man I am
Back from hell and out on the road of life again
This is me, glad to say, finally on my way

This is me, I am real.

OCEAN DREAM

Caught in a trap, dirty streets and no return
Tenement blocks as final destination
Caught in a lie that I will have time to burn
When the creditors declare their assertion
Crouched on a couch, I eked out my existence
Time after time I sank into oblivion
Dreams over board, broken mind in close distance
Everything`s lost of its signification

Disillusion and denounced as hardship case
Every night out on the street to booze it up
Drawn in the past, no chance to tie up my lace
Drunken nights with the mates in a run-down pub
Burned-out and broke, numb on the brink of ruin
Nothing to lose and hooked up in a night club
Tired and weak, no strength for a better begin
With accident the light of my life lit up
(And now)

I`m on my way and it gonna be alright
Gonna feel like a virgin
I`m on my way and don`t wanna pick a fight
Wanna live my ocean dream
I`m on my way and it gonna be alright
Gonna make it urgent
I`m on my way and don`t wanna pick a fight
Wanna live my ocean dream

Cotched in the park, got rat-arsed nearly all day
And the off days we spent smoking a bong
Nicked and got bombed, we tried to shag every bay
And had a fag to make our lives chug along
(But now)

I`m on my way and it gonna be alright

Gonna feel like a virgin
I`m on my way and don`t wanna pick a fight
Wanna live my ocean dream
I`m on my way and it gonna be alright
Gonna make it urgent
I`m on my way and don`t wanna pick a fight
Wanna live my ocean dream

WHAT MADE THEM DO IT?

Ah, I can't make it another day
Enough's enough, it gonna break me
Hour after hour the same shit way
No-one above who wanna wake me!
Darkness, yeah, blindness behind the mask
How can you let them shake me, fake me
Like a monster without any task,
Come on, say why they wanna hate me?

What made them do it?
Couldn't they see that they rob my illusion?
Made me spend my day in confusion?
What made them do it?
Didn't they know that they damage my integration?
Made me exile from my destination?
What made them do it?
How couldn't you know it!

Ah, disguise in the masquerade,
Too much's too much, it will defeat me
Day after day the same old shade,
Can't get in touch, who wanna eat me!
Lonesome, yeah, boredom behind the light,
Why did you let them beat me, cheat me
Like a wild boar hunted in the night,
Explain, why they wanna delete me?

What made them do it?
Couldn't they see that they rob my illusion?
Made me spend my day in confusion?
What made them do it?
Didn't they know that they damage my integration?
Made me exile from my destination?
What made them do it?
How couldn't you know it!

A kick in the groin, what made them do it?
A hit in the face, what made them do it?
How couldn't you know it!

WOULD IT BE A CRIME?

Don`t be late, don`t hesitate
As long as you put your shoes under our table
Be polite, be home at night
Oh man, can you tell me how I will be able
To follow those strange rules into a better life
When I don`t get a space where I can feel alive?

Would it be a crime to break out of confusion?
Would it be a crime to stop the human convulsion
To present the final solution?

It would be a crime when we don`t find a way
To live in peace and harmony
It would be a crime when we can`t waste a day
To create our own fantasy
It would be a crime when we won`t find our bay!

Tell the truth, lace up your shoes
As long as you`re with us stay out of a taproom
Pack your bag, don`t look back
Oh man, tell me how I will get rid of that gloom
To face this never-ending trouble-making truth
Without losing what everyone is calling youth?

Would it be a crime to believe in our creation?
Would it be a crime to bring us in a relation
To see our planet as one nation?

It would be a crime when we don`t catch our bliss
To live in peace and harmony
It would be a crime when we can`t waste a kiss
To fulfill our own fantasy
It would be a crime when we won`t try to live!

Would it be a crime to look for someone special?

Would it be a crime to stop keeping our minds racial
Because our life`s international?

It would be a crime when we don`t cash our dream
To live in peace and harmony
It would be a crime when we can`t lead the beam
To present our own fantasy
It would be a crime when we won`t be a team!

THAT BOY

He's gonna shopping, life's gonna popping
Out in the mall, he let the girls be bobbing
No need to pay cash; annsummers ain't trash
Let everyone know, he can't make a hash
He's gonna showing, his budget's growing
Out for the show, he let the money flowing
He's Dan, the ban of man, where girls wanna dash!

I will be standing, he'll be falling
You don't wanna fuck with me!
On facebook and on msn
They talk about that boy, Burk-in-show!
And I'll be standing, you'll be crawling
You don't wanna fuck with me!
From bearshare out to every den
They talk about that boy, Burk-in-show!

He's gonna strolling, let jewels rolling
Home in the net, he let the card exploding
He uses a wrong name; it won't be his shame
Everyone would bet, he can't fool the game
He's gonna moping, his credit's sloping
Out for a shaq, he needs Amazon for groping
He's Dan, the ban of man, whose friends wanna blame!

I will be standing, he'll be falling
You don't wanna fuck with me!
On facebook and on msn
They talk about that boy, Burk-in-show!
And I'll be standing, you'll be crawling
You don't wanna fuck with me!
From bearshare out to every den
They talk about that boy, Burk-in-show!

They talk about that boy on the scene

The surfboard behind the screen
They talk about that boy with blond hair
The virus in the hardware
They talk about that boy on facebook,
That boy with the strange look!

I will be standing, he'll be falling
You don't wanna fuck with me!
On facebook and on msn
They talk about that boy, Burk-in-show!
And I'll be standing, you'll be crawling
You don't wanna fuck with me!
From bearshare out to every den
They talk about that boy, Burk-in-show!

BLOOD ON BLOOD

When the world is crashing in a terrible sound
And you think your body will smash up on the ground
What do you think, who will be there waiting for you?
When the bright colors of the world are fading out
And the pressure of the air will make you fall down
What do you think, who will be there waiting for you?

History shows again and again
Absolutely nothing feels better than
Blood on blood!
History shows again and again
Absolutely nothing feels better than
Blood on blood!

When the world you know is caught in a heavy storm
And your best buddy will put you out of the dorm
What do you think, who will be there, waiting for you?
When the wide world lets you know, you are out of norm
And there is no other place for you in the form
What do you think, who will be there, waiting for you?

History shows again and again
Absolutely nothing feels better than
Blood on blood!
History shows again and again
Absolutely nothing feels better than
Blood on blood!

That's the lesson we could have learned from old Rome
If we'd only turned the page of the ancient tome
All except our own blood is made of loam and foam!

History shows again and again
Absolutely nothing feels better than
Blood on blood!

History shows again and again
Absolutely nothing feels better than
Blood on blood!

Absolutely nothing feels better than
Blood on blood!

MY PATH

Back from hell, living in paradise
With Eden Cove straight on the other side
Turned the wheel, followed my own dusty path
That led me out of the family mess
Once I was caught in an adult made cage
Like so many kids who are under age

But I never stopped, I never ever stopped dreaming
And now, here I am, still wandering on my path
Yeah, I never stopped, I never ever stopped dreaming
And now, I'm a man, still wandering on his path

Back in life, working in my leisure
With guidance from friends all over the earth
Turned the page, discovered another culture
That gave me back the holy nature's worth
Once I was caught in a survival fight
Like so many men who can't reach the light

But I never stopped, I never ever stopped dreaming
And now, here I am, still wandering on my path
Yeah, I never stopped, I never ever stopped dreaming
And now, I'm a man, still wandering on his path

Bienvenue a l'ile Maurice,
Bienvenue dans le monde des miracles

But I never stopped, I never ever stopped dreaming
And now, here I am, still wandering on my path
Yeah, I never stopped, I never ever stopped dreaming
And now, I'm a man, still wandering on his path

ANGEL OF THE PAST

Long time ago I served drinks and cold snacks,
Was everybody`s sunshine
But then I grew up and the angel I used to be
Ran out of time
Blame all on me, I don`t care, but better be aware
The angel of the past is the devil of today
The angel of the past is the devil of today

Then, as grown-up this old lady gave me a ride
Back to my abode
Telling me that I`m a disgrace and the angel
May give me a thought
I simply gave up the ghost, got drawn in the lost
The angel of the past is the devil of today
The angel of the past is the devil of today

Another night, another drive and nothing had changed
May the angel guide me on the way to his range
Her faith became her fate, sending postcards her trade
The angel of the past is the devil of today
The angel of the past is the devil of today

BEHIND THE SMILE

My life has taken me beyond all imaginations
Made me rise and fall, tore me apart
But have you ever seen it in a relation
To what was hidden in my heart
How many nights I've been hunted by the past?

They say they gave me a better chance in life
But who knows what the future may bring
They say their choice gave me a chance to survive
But for me it really meant nothing!

Behind the smile hides a crying face
A childhood like none should be!

My life often has cut me off from the society around
Discouraged me, made me crack up
Have you ever known how it feels to be aground
To discuss your pain in a hub
To be a member of the alien club?

They say they love me, but I can't see the truth
It's all buried deep in my soul
They say they saved me from my family blues
But who asked them to take control?

Behind the smile hides a crying face
A childhood like none should be!

A MONKEY IN THE MUSIC

I'm on my way back, burning like never before
Working on new tracks, wanna give my best and more
'Cause this is my time and I'm ready for the flight
All will be fine, expectations may be high
But I'm on my way, can feel the rhythm inside
So let come what may, I'll be ready to fight!

I'm nothing but a monkey in the music
And I am totally lost in here
Nothing but a monkey in the music
Can survive in such an atmosphere
Living in empty spaces
Looking at empty faces
Visiting different places
Feeding the different races
I am nothing
Nothing but a monkey in the music!

I'm gonna return, nothing's gonna stop me now
With all what I learn and the old stuff that I know
'Cause my time has come, the best won't be good enough
Shining like the sun, with poems written by love
This time it will burn, nothing's gonna stop me now!

I'm nothing but a monkey in the music
And I am totally lost in here
Nothing but a monkey in the music
Can survive in such an atmosphere
Living in a twilight
Shaking up all the rights
Giving up the good night
Doing everything right
I am nothing
Nothing but a monkey in the music!
But I am I am a monkey in the music!

SON OF HAMBURG

Gotta let everyone know, proudly presented right now:

I'm a cool-calculating, brown-white son of Hamburg
Who doesn't like some proud suburb-bastards around
When he enjoys his Astra-beer and goes out in the
atmosphere!
I'm a non-profit-making, brown-white son of Hamburg!

The hell bells ring and the saints come marching in,
Tonight's the night and we know Pauli will win.
Cheering and praying, fearing and saying
Tonight's the night and then later on the mile
We celebrate our brown and white party isle!
Gotta let them know, gotta do it now:

I'm a cool-calculating, brown-white son of Hamburg
Who doesn't like some proud suburb-bastards around
When he enjoys his Astra-beer and goes out in the
atmosphere!
I'm a non-profit-making, brown-white son of Hamburg!

Well, nobody wins against the boys in brown,
This is the match that never will be unknown.
Cheering and praying, fearing and saying
This is the match no-one will ever forget
With all the high-rising hopes and fears we had.
Gonna kick it in, gonna make us win!

I'm a cool-calculating, brown-white son of Hamburg
Who doesn't like some proud suburb-bastards around
When he enjoys his Astra-beer and goes out in the
atmosphere!
I'm a non-profit-making, brown-white son of Hamburg!

Well, some call us chum and some may call us bum

But we're the ones, who fight against the Nazi scum,
Cheering and praying, fearing and saying
We are the ones, well-suited in brown and white
And support our Saint Pauli through every tide!
Gotta let them know, gotta do it now:

I'm a cool-calculating, brown-white son of Hamburg
Who doesn't like some proud suburb-bastards around
When he enjoys his Astra-beer and goes out in the
atmosphere!
I'm a non-profit-making, brown-white son of Hamburg!

LIFE'S TOO SHORT

Well, I have to turn the page, the last of my life
See the things I went through without you by my side
All the good days, bad days I could survive
It's over and gone now, travelling into the light

Lucky was the moment
You crossed the borderline
To bring back one
Last love into my darkest time
So that the sun started to shine!

Life's too short;
Have you seen my last emotion?
Gave all till the end of my day
Life's too short;
To waste your time in devotion!
I thought till the end of my way!

Three words, two hearts,
One night is all I was made for.
Three words, two hearts,
One love will give us so much more
That's what I haven't known before!

Life's too short;
Have you seen my last emotion?
Gave all till the end of my day
Life's too short;
To waste your time in devotion!
I thought till the end of my way!

PART TWO

Starting Something

STARTING SOMETHING...
AGAIN

Would you come out and play with me?

Two years of brainstorming, scribbling, and frustration, and here we are. Nothing turned out like I'd planned, not even in my wildest dreams—but in the end, it turned out better than I could have imagined. This collection? It's born from the chaos of 9/11, wars raging around the world, and me just trying to figure out how to be an adult in a life that seemed to be falling apart.

Back in 2001, I tried picking up the pen again after an 18-month break. But those four songs I wrote? They didn't even convince me I still had it in me. The words weren't flowing, the writer's block was suffocating, and I was barely keeping it together. I'd dropped out of school, couldn't find a job, had no clue what my future was going to look like. It was a rough time, and creativity? Yeah, that was dead in the water.

Then, in late 2000, I made a decision that changed everything. All my life, I swore I'd never move to Hamburg. And yet, come September, I had no choice. I lost the only home I'd ever known and tumbled from one problem to the next. Every time I thought I'd hit rock bottom, the floor gave way again.

I bounced from job to job, sharing a tiny, crappy apartment with my alcoholic biological dad, and eventually found myself homeless. It took six long months to scrape together enough to get my own place. Finally, summer of 2001, I moved into a small apartment in a sketchy neighborhood everyone warned me about. No one thought I'd last there—and, honestly, neither did I. I hated it. For years, I tried to escape that place.

My future looked bleak. No creativity, buried in drugs, booze, and depression—my life was going nowhere. And then 9/11 happened.

Like everyone else, I was shell-shocked by those images. But after a while, fear set in. Fear, and a deep sense of unease watching how politicians and corporations were milking this tragedy for their own gain. And then, Hamburg—the city I never wanted to live in—became a key part of the story. The attacks were planned here, practically in my backyard. Some of those guys even lived near me. I felt guilty, like everyone else around here, but I refused to blame Islam for what happened.

I grew a beard. Not as a protest, not to provoke anyone, just to show solidarity with Muslims who were facing hatred. I never expected the backlash I got. Bus drivers wouldn't let me on, people moved away from me on the train, and I could see the fear in their eyes. I got a taste of what it's like to be an outsider, to feel like you don't belong in your own city.

I thought Hamburg was tolerant. I was wrong. That rejection only deepened my depression, but somehow it also sparked something in me. It made me think, reflect, and then... the writer's block lifted.

I can't explain how it happened, but by the end of 2001, I had this idea—a new project that would tie together my past and everything going on around me. In February 2002, I finally wrote the first lyrics. I told myself I'd write one song a day, but then it just poured out of me. I wrote Too Much Stuff, Would You Come Out and Play with Me, and Sell Her Soul to the Devil in a single day, with two more half-finished. For the first time in a long time, I felt alive again.

But as quickly as it came, that spark burned out. The next day, nothing. And it stayed that way for the rest of the year.

By October, I was at rock bottom, seriously considering ending it all. But at the last second, something shifted, and I got pulled back from the edge. That was the real turning point. Suddenly, things started to fall into place. The line "Get it in your head, I am the living dead" popped into my mind, and I wrote Starting Something. More lyrics followed, and for the first time in years,

I started to believe in myself again. I realized that if I worked hard enough, maybe I did have a future as a writer.

The truth is, life was never going to be easy for me. No poet's life ever is. But the dream wasn't dead, and I was willing to fight for it.

I didn't write every day, but when the creativity hit, I grabbed it. In 2002, I had two major writing sessions, and in 2003, three more. That's how I finished what I started—the project that eventually became STARTING SOMETHING.

But as soon as I felt like it was done, the writer's block came back, hitting me like a freight train. This time, it felt like it was for good. After a few years of fighting it, I decided to let go of the dream. I buried it and moved on, trying to build a new life that didn't involve writing. And just when I did, that's when my creativity came back. Just one song, written during the 2006 World Cup—Leader of a Hooligan Fight. I saved the file and moved on.

Looking back now, I can see that Starting Something was the turning point. It was the moment I finally grew up and started living the life I was meant to live.

(Hamburg, Germany, 2009)

Christian Bass

STARTING SOMETHING

Close to midnight and something's creaking on the floor
Lurking in the dark, waiting behind every door
There's nothing else to do
Well their time has come, blood is upon the carpet
So tell me what ghoul is living in your apartment
When someone's watching you

You better run, you better do what you can
Or this would be the end of your life
It's not your friend, you better fear that demon
Don't be tough if you wanna survive

I am the living dead, so get it in your head
I wanna be starting something
And it doesn't matter who's wrong or right
I'm gonna be starting something
And it doesn't matter who's wrong or right
So get it in your head: I am the living dead!

There's a glow behind your window, a howl in the night
And a grumble under your bed, nothing is right
Blood traces in the hall
A foulest stench is in the air, they're out to find
Yeah, can't you see the creatures creeping up behind
And hear, the dead man call

You better run, you better do what you can
Or this would be the end of your life
I am not your friend, you better fear my hand
Don't be tough and you will stay alive

I am the living dead, so get it in your head
I wanna be starting something
And it doesn't matter who's wrong or right
I'm gonna be starting something

And it doesn't matter who's wrong or right
So get it in your head: I am the living dead!

I'm watching you when you sleep
When you're down I'm underneath!

WOULD YOU COME OUT...

Ha-ha, ho-ho, what do you wanna do?
Something's going down,
Try to get your chance and kick it, too!

Time after time I gave her all of my money
Worked day by day for her old cold words of honey
I lay all my faith in her and left my girlfriend
'Cause she promised me that she will leave her husband
But it was only a play right up in her league
And then she shot the game and made me really sick!

Oh, when you wanna survive
Show me what you gonna do
'Cause I'll get your ass dead or alive
Oh, why you don't make me proud
Show me that your words were true
'Cause I'll come in when you don't come out!

Would you come out and play with me?
Would you come out and play with me?
Would you come out and play with me?
Wouldn't you?
Wouldn't you?

Night after night she called me to say words of love
And I thought she could show me the heaven above
But all what that woman did was kicking me down
So she made me be a monkey with a crown
I don't know how often she lied her kids were sick
Just everything was a play right up in her league

Oh, when you wanna survive
Show me what you gonna do
'Cause I'll get your ass dead or alive
Oh, why you don't make me proud

Show me that your words were true
'Cause I'll come in when you don't come out!

Would you come out and play with me?
Would you come out and play with me?
Would you come out and play with me?
Wouldn't you?
Wouldn't you?

Ha-ha, ho-ho, what do you wanna do?
Something's going down,
Try to get your chance and kick it, too!

SELL HER SOUL TO THE DEVIL

She hit me when I wasn't her mind
And just all of her friends were blind
To see the whole need I lived in
Against her I couldn't win
She really tried to kill my way
And she tried to cruel me every day

Before you judge me
Try hard to understand me
She dug a ditch, she's every lick

So you better sell her soul to the devil
She's in love with the forces of evil
Why you don't sell her soul to the devil
She's fucking with the forces of evil

She played a game of greed and lust
And begged me to give her my trust
With violence, she broke my door
Privacy I just had no more
She really tried to thrill my way
And she tried to cruel me every day

Before you judge me
Try hard to understand me
She's a hot bitch and makes me sick

So you better sell her soul to the devil
She's in love with the forces of evil
Why you don't sell her soul to the devil
She's fucking with the forces of evil

With the terror she made me mad
And she locked me in my own flat
Told everybody I'm not home

So that I just was all alone
And that is why I've disappeared
To be lonely was all I feared

Before you judge me
Try hard to understand me
She dug a ditch, she's every lick

So you better sell her soul to the devil
She's in love with the forces of evil
Why you don't sell her soul to the devil
She's fucking with the forces of evil

Before you judge me
Try hard to understand me
She's a hot bitch and makes me sick

So you better sell her soul to the devil
She's in love with the forces of evil
Why you don't sell her soul to the devil
She's fucking with the forces of evil

Come on spare me her lies
So many tears have left my eyes
There won't be one more chance
Although we are all no saints!

TOO MUCH STUFF

Aren't these pictures enough
To face the problems now?
It's not about true love
When you're caught in a show
There will be no way out
In the league of weak shouts
You will take more of what you had
Next day you want it twice as bad

They're lurking in the park
And they play with your life
They'll tear you in the dark
Give you cuts like a knife

Before you put it in
Close your eyes and count to ten!
It ain't - it ain't too much stuff
It ain't - it ain't too much to stay alive!
It ain't - ain't too much stuff
It ain't - it ain't too much to kill your life!
You better stop it when you wanna survive!

You will stalk on the run
If you cannot raise the money
And you will lose your fun
Don't take this shit honey!
Why do you want the buzz?
There's not another drug
Come on, lose your control
The devil wants your soul!

You better leave the scene
When you wanna stay alive!
So don't give up your dream
With that you can't survive!

Before you put it in
Close your eyes and count to ten!
It ain't - it ain't too much stuff
It ain't - it ain't too much to stay alive!
It ain't - ain't too much stuff
It ain't - it ain't too much to kill your life!

They're lurking in the park
And they play with your life
They'll tear you in the dark
Give you cuts like a knife
Why do you want the buzz?
You better gimme your trust!

Before you put it in
Close your eyes and count to ten!
It ain't - it ain't too much stuff
It ain't - it ain't too much to stay alive!
It ain't - ain't too much stuff
It ain't - it ain't too much to kill your life!
You better stop it when you wanna survive!

BORN TO LOSE

Streets are burning under my shoes
The sky's dark and rain's coming down
Blue feeling inside, nothing else to do
When I walk along the road to town

Hearts of stone – we were born to lose
From the cradle to the grave
There is no heaven, baby, that's the truth
Just betrayed and sold like a slave
Yeah baby, we were born to lose

Late at night when the moon rises up
And drives away the darkness
Baby you will know that we leave the club
And try to learn know the art of madness

Face-to-face – we were born to lose
From the heaven to a hell
There's no justice, baby, that's the truth
We'll betray and sell for the well
Yeah baby, we were born to lose

Tears and fears – we were born to lose
From a junkie to a chief
Just no paradise, baby, that's the blues
Where we're haunted like a thief
So baby, we were born to lose

WAITING FOR THE DAY

Nothing to smoke, nothing to eat
The dark sun's on the rise
Trees on fire when the autumn comes
The dark sun's on the rise
Nothing to drink in that dry heat
The dark sun's on the rise
Waiting on the last burning sun
When the devil's inside

I'm waiting - waiting for the day
Waiting for the day to move away
Gonna chase the thunderstorm away
I'm waiting - waiting for the day
Waiting for the day to move away
Wanna make the paradise to stay

Nothing to work, nothing to live
We remain worlds apart
The heaven's ringing the flag down
We remain worlds apart
Nothing to fear, nothing to miss
We remain worlds apart
Crowded together in a town
United in our hearts

I'm waiting - waiting for the day
Waiting for the day to move away
Gonna chase the thunderstorm away
I'm waiting - waiting for the day
Waiting for the day to move away
Wanna make the paradise to stay

Gonna keep the faith and pray
Wanna keep the faith to stay
Gonna keep the faith and pray

Wanna keep the faith today

I'm waiting - waiting for the day
Waiting for the day to move away
Gonna chase the thunderstorm away
I'm waiting - waiting for the day
Waiting for the day to move away
Wanna make the paradise to stay

WHO WANTS WHO?

At first it seemed to me like it was true love
Gave him everything inside one heart could be found
And too late, I realized that it wasn't enough
So tell me now how often his best friend came around?

He played a game, he broke my heart
And he thought I wouldn't notice it!
He took my soul, tore it apart
And he thought I wouldn't notice it!

Who wants who, who needs you
Boy, there is nothing else to do
No time to ignore it, we'll come to the end!
Who wants who, he loves you
And believe me, his love is true
But there's no way, boy, just no way to stay friends!

He was more than a beauty queen of the scene
But then I realized that he only made a show
Just everything looked like in a sparkling dream
And when I saw them sleeping: it is all over now!

He played a game, he broke my heart
And he thought I wouldn't notice it!
He took my soul, tore it apart
And he thought I wouldn't notice it!

Who wants who, who needs you
Boy, there is nothing else to do
No time to ignore it, we'll come to the end!
Who wants who, he loves you
And believe me, his love is true
But there's no way, boy, just no way to stay friends!

WHERE MY FRIENDS ARE

When the red sun is fading out
And the old moon is rising up
I can hear my old classmates shout
When the red sun is fading out
I am standing here with my gout
While my old friends enter the night club

Working for the Co
Time's moving slow
Working from nine to five
No way to be alive

There's a sound jamming in my ears
Because Friday night is here
And I wanna be where my friends are
I wanna be where my friends are
Where my friends are
I wanna be where my friends are
They're out to have fun this night
And I cannot be on their side

Slowly the hours are passing by
Waiting for my life to begin
No break, no mind, a man doesn't cry
Slowly the hours are passing by
Sweating until I have to die
There is no chance for me to win
Slowly the hours are passing by
Waiting for my life to begin

Working for the state
Till it's too late
Working from nine to five
No way to be alive

There's a sound jamming in my ears
Because Friday night is here
And I wanna be where my friends are
I wanna be where my friends are
Where my friends are
I wanna be where my friends are
They're out to have fun this night
And I cannot be on their side

Sweating in the hall
No life at all
Sweating from nine to five
No way to survive

There's a sound jamming in my ears
Because Friday night is here
And I wanna be where my friends are
I wanna be where my friends are
Where my friends are
I wanna be where my friends are
They're out to have fun this night
And I cannot be on their side

EMPTY ROOM

I woke up this morning in my dead man's suit
Under a cold burning neon sun
A new day was dawning to show the whole need
When the congregation is gone
I woke up and wanted to chase the clouds away
I woke up and wanted to chase the clouds away

Empty room, empty room
I woke up this morning in an empty room!
Empty room, empty room
I stood up this morning in a bloody doom!

There is blood on the streets where our children walk
On a dusty and dirty road
Not a single heartbeat where emptiness talks
When the whole world's overloaded
I stood up and wanted to make this world to stay
I stood up and wanted to make this world to stay

Empty room, empty room
I woke up this morning in an empty room!
Empty room, empty room
I stood up this morning in a bloody doom!

BLOOD ON THE PLAYGROUND

You hear the back door slam
Can hear his voice in the air
You're working for his meal
School's over and he's not there
You're waiting for so long
You're waiting in vain
But your kid will never come again!

He got your baby
And he knows your name
He drives you crazy
It's just no game

That man got your baby
And that man ain't your friend
Look who drives you crazy,
Why it can't have an end?
Blood is on the playground,
Blood is on the slide
That man got your baby
And that man held you tight

You see his smiling face
Can hear his laughter outside
You're cleaning his left place
School's over, but nothing's right
You're waiting for so long
You're waiting in vain
But your kid will never come again!

He killed your baby
And he knew you care
He drove you crazy
It's just not fair

That man got your baby
And that man ain't your friend
Look who drives you crazy
Why it can't have an end?
Blood is on the playground
Blood is on the slide
That man got your baby
And that man held you tight

But the officer said
Everything will be okay
He's playing with a friend
This would happen every day
But you know:

That man got your baby
And that man ain't your friend
Look who drives you crazy
Why it can't have an end?
Blood is on the playground,
Blood is on the slide
That man got your baby
And that man held you tight

Blood is on the playground
Blood is on the slide
(Keep it in the closet)
Blood is on the playground
Blood is on the slide
(Keep it, just keep it)
Blood is on the playground
Blood is on the slide
And I can't take it no more!

BATES MOTEL

She's driving on the highway
Rain is coming down
She knows nothing is okay
Since she left the town
All her friends are far away
Living their life at home
But she had to leave this bay
And now she's all alone

Red letters on the horizon
Waiting for tired runaways
Just telling them they're welcome
Telling them here you can stay

Because you're welcome
You're just welcome in Bates Motel
Come on, you're welcome
We've a lot of bodies for sale!
Don't forget you're welcome
You're just welcome in Bates Motel
Come on, you're welcome
We've a lot of bodies for sale!

He's riding on his black bike
Along the main street
Thinking about things he likes
Stepping to the beat
There's a thing he can't leave behind
Flickering in his brain
And this thing will cruel his mind
He can't get rid of this pain

Red letters on the horizon
Waiting for tired runaways
Just telling them they're welcome

Telling them here you can stay

Because you're welcome
You're just welcome in Bates Motel
Come on, you're welcome
We've a lot of bodies for sale!
Don't forget you're welcome
You're just welcome in Bates Motel
Come on, you're welcome
We've a lot of bodies for sale!

Big letters on the horizon
Promise you sunny temptation
And you know that you are welcome
In that lonely heart club nation

Because you're welcome
You're just welcome in Bates Motel
Come on, you're welcome
We've a lot of bodies for sale!
Don't forget you're welcome
You're just welcome in Bates Motel
Come on, you're welcome
We've a lot of bodies for sale!
Come on baby, you're welcome
You're just welcome in Bates Motel!

GONE TOO SOON

For my Grandparents!

Starlight
Shining so bright from a distance
And love will be the last message
Lonely
You are feeling deep in your heart
There'll never be another part

Can you tell me
Why, why everything is gone too soon?
Why, why everybody will rise with the moon?
Please answer me
Why, why everybody will have such a doom?
Why, why everything is gone too soon?

Starlight
Sending its light from a paradise
To fetch our souls for a last rise
Weakness
Will be the feeling deep inside
When a day is fading to a night

Can you tell me
Why, why everything is gone too soon?
Why, why everybody will rise with the moon?
Please answer me
Why, why everybody will have such a doom?
Why, why everything is gone too soon?

LEADERS OF A HOOLIGAN FIGHT

It happened in the nineties we were young and proud
When we knew there wouldn't be such a night.
They were gods, we were better, so come on shout it out
We were the winners of a hooligan fight!
We were the winners of a hooligan fight!

So much stronger than before
We've caught them out on the floor
So what? So what?
And after the day passed through
We did what we had to do
So what? So what?

It was back in the nineties we were young and proud
When we knew there wouldn't be such a night
They were good, we were better, so come on shout it out
We were the leaders of a hooligan fight!
We were the leaders of a hooligan fight!

We weren't jealous of the kids
When we swung our iron fists
So what? So what?
We fought with blood in our face
Kicked them all over the place
So what? So what?

It was back in the nineties we were young and proud
When we knew there wouldn't be such a night
They were good, we were better, so come on shout it out
We were the leaders of a hooligan fight!
We were the leaders of a hooligan fight!

Red cross on white ground
We waved our banner all over the place

Bad thoughts on good sound
We kicked them down on knees, brothers of rage

It was back in the nineties we were young and proud
When we knew there wouldn't be such a night
They were good, we were better, so come on shout it out
We were the leaders of a hooligan fight!
We were the leaders of a hooligan fight!

Burned down the ground, threw some Molotov cocktails
And side by side, we went straight into the jail!

It happened in the nineties we were young and proud
When we knew there wouldn't be such a night.
They were gods, we were better, so come on shout it loud
We were the winners of a hooligan fight!
We were the winners of a hooligan fight!

CAN'T YOU SEE THE MISERY?

Mother's cry
Because their babies die
This is the thing I've to tell

White doves fly
And our presidents lie
Mother earth ain't feeling well

Out on the street
See kids with not enough to eat
Old dirty clothes
With no shoes on their feet

Tell me, can't you see?
Can't you see the misery?

Bombs fall down
Kill the life on the ground
Hard swords about nature's worth

Crying clown
When they burn out the town
And no-one believes in his church

Out on the street
See kids with not enough to eat
Old dirty clothes
With no shoes on their feet

Tell me, can't you see?
Can't you see the misery?

Many children have nothing to eat
And they wear no shoes on their feet
Saw hungry eyes in different faces

There's no humanity between the races
And too much violence on the street
Our planet earth has a big demand
And our presidents cannot understand
Those soldiers always suppress the weak
So we have to face such problems now
And to finish this major freak show

Tell me, can't you see?
Can't you see the misery?

Out on the street
See kids with not enough to eat
Old dirty clothes
With no shoes on their feet

Tell me, can't you see?
Can't you see the misery?

ABOUT THE AUTHOR

Christian Bass was born in September 1978 in Hamburg, northern Germany, and grew up in Ahrensburg. From 2009 to 2015, he called the beautiful island of Mauritius home. Since then, he's been living and working in Essen, West Germany— but in 2024, he made the move back to Mauritius. Christian studied journalism and digital photography at ILS Hamburg, dove into audiovisual psychology at Yale University, and sharpened his skills in persuasive rhetoric at Harvard University.

His passion for writing began early, kicking off in 1988 when he started crafting poetry and short stories. Just 11 years later, he had his first publication, and more would follow over time. Between 2000 and 2002, Christian's work made its way into numerous magazines, particularly erotic short stories and poems in various anthologies. But it wasn't until 2011 that his career truly took off. That's when he founded cbvisions photography, turning his passion into a dream come true.

Since then, Christian has been unstoppable, with numerous publications under his belt. His body of work spans poems, lyrics, short stories, novels, and even compositions, written in German, English, and sometimes in French and Spanish. With a creative fire that shows no sign of slowing, Christian Bass continues to make his mark across genres and languages, sharing his unique voice with the world.

#

Thank you for reading my poetry. If you enjoyed it, won't you please take a moment to leave me a review at your favorite retailer? Thank you for helping me in making my dream come true!

Yours sincerely
Christian Bass